The Common Sense Guide to Purchasing a Home in Good Times and Bad

Including Bonus Credit Chapter

Written by

Dan Craddock

DISCLAIMERS and ACKNOWLEDGEMENTS

At the time of writing, the author is a licensed Realtor® in the states of California, DRE #01907845, and Florida, SL3211308, and is not providing any advice on Real Estate other than his own opinions. Please consult a professional Realtor® for specific information on purchasing a home in your area.

The author is NOT an Attorney. The material in this book is for informational purposes only and not for the purpose of providing legal advice. You should contact your attorney to obtain advice with respect to any particular issue, problem or situation. The opinions of the author may not reflect the opinions of an attorney and should not be construed as legal advice.

Copyright Notice

ACKNOWLEDGEMENTS

This book is dedicated to my wife Linda who has encouraged me to be creative and follow my passion.

Table of Contents

Contents

CHAPTER 1

INTRODUCTION

"In the middle of every difficulty lies opportunity" - **Albert Einstein**

This common sense approach to purchasing a home will provide you with all the information you need to go out there and confidently purchase a home whether it be your dream home, a second home or an investment property. This guide is written in common sense language for everyone to understand so that you can be in the top 20% of knowledgeable home buyers. You owe it to yourself to become as knowledgeable as you can.

Purchasing a home is probably the biggest and scariest decision that you will make in your entire lifetime. Yes, it is scary and yes it does have huge consequences. In the past, the advice given was to purchase the most home that you can afford given your current resources. Over time, the more expensive the house was the more money you would eventually make on the resale of the house. This theory has proven itself time after time over the course of the last 50 years up until the housing bust which began in 2006. It is impossible to predict issues like job loss, health problems, divorce or other catastrophic events that could turn your investment sour. As a result, the housing bust combined with the economic downturn has flipped this theory upside down. The new theory is to purchase what you like at the price you can afford.

This guide was written to provide potential homebuyers with the necessary information to move forward and not get taken advantage of. In addition, this guide will explain why purchasing a home should not be done without utilizing the resources at your disposal. There are many people that you will need during the process and this guide will let you know when they are needed and how to get the most out of them.

After reading this guide, you will have all the information you need to make an informed decision and the process will actually be FUN which is what we all need more of in our lives. An informed buyer is a happy buyer. Good Luck and may your journey be an enjoyable and profitable one.

CHAPTER 2

WHEN IS THE BEST TIME TO BUY?

"Real Estate is at the core of almost every business, and it's certainly at the core of most people's wealth. In order to build your wealth and improve your business smarts, you need to know about Real Estate." – **Donald Trump**

I believe every home buyer has asked themselves this question over and over again and the truth of the matter is that the answer is different for everyone. Yes, there are certainly better times to buy but not everyone is in a position to or wants to wait for those times to come around. Things happen in our lives that are beyond our control and we have to make decisions based on our current situation.

If the decision to buy was purely a financial one then the answer would be easier and apply almost across the board. However, the answer is not purely financial. It is also based on life events and necessity. If you are a typical single family homeowner and your personal situation dictates that you need to move or it makes sense for you to move then you're likely to move to another single family home no matter whether it is the best time to buy or not. From a financial standpoint, it typically makes more sense to purchase rather than to rent since we can still take advantage of the home mortgage interest deduction. However, we need to be prudent about our decision and approach it not only from an emotional standpoint but a logical one as well.

Emotion is a powerful force. It tells us to purchase exactly what we want when we want it. This is the how most home buyers purchase a home. They buy on emotion and attempt to justify the decision with logic. Logic tells us to purchase when home prices and interest rates are low. Logic also tells us to purchase a house that is neither the biggest nor the smallest one in the neighborhood. Logic also tells us to purchase in a great neighborhood with the best schools, close to shopping, close to a firehouse, away from busy streets, etc. If the decision were purely logical then it would be relatively straightforward and easy, but we all know that lifestyle is the most important driver. Happiness is the key driver and if you're not happy with your purchase then it's not a good one. If you purchase a home purely because of logic and forget the emotional component then your purchase will surely cause you problems in the long run.

Let's discuss the market and the economy and how this enters into the purchase decision.

Historically, buying a home was looked upon as an investment rather than just a place to live. Many people looked at their home as their retirement nest egg. They were going to retire and sell their home to fund their retirement. Well, reality has set in. Your personal home is **NOT AN INVESTMENT!** Yes, it has the potential but we can't expect it nor count on it to provide returns that rival the stock and bond markets. In fact, home price appreciation has barely exceeded inflation over long periods of time. Your home is for you and your family to live in and that's what you should purchase it for.

We never would have predicted that home prices would go down as much as they have. In addition, we never would have predicted that our economy would go into a recession and stay depressed for such a long period of time. Things do happen in life that we aren't prepared for and we just have to make the best of the situation.

Although the economic climate is bad and unemployment is high, there are factors working in our favor. Interest rates are at historic lows which mean that we can purchase more home for the dollar. In other words, with 30 year fixed rate mortgage rates under 4%, you qualify for a larger mortgage and thus a more expensive home than if the mortgage rate where at the historical average of 8%. In addition, home prices are at their lowest level in years. In southwest Florida, home prices have dropped so much that a builder can't build a home for what he can buy one for now. The term we use is replacement cost. It's a great time to buy when you can purchase a previously owned home for far less than the cost of purchasing a new home.

Logic tells us that it's the right time to buy when prices are at the bottom of the cycle or on the rise. It is, in fact, a buyers' market in many parts of the country right now. Areas such as southwest Florida, Nevada and Arizona still have elevated supplies of homes resulting in lower competition among buyers and, thus, lower prices. However, there are other parts of the country, such as northern California where inventory is at historical lows and homes are getting 20 to 30 offers above the asking prices.

So when is the right time to buy? While factors such as home prices and mortgage rates have an obvious bearing on the answer to this question, the true answer is unique to each buyer. If your financial situation and lifestyle are supportive of your desire to purchase a home, then now is the time to buy. Otherwise, your best course of action might be to formulate a plan to get your financial and personal state of affairs aligned with your goal of home ownership.

CHAPTER 3

WHAT DO I DO FIRST?

*"Life is one grand, sweet song, so start the music." – **Ronald Reagan***

Now that you've determined that it's time to take the plunge, I'll outline the process and what you should be doing first. You've probably searched the internet for homes in the area that you want to buy in and most likely have searched for your ideal home maybe on the water or with a pool or close to great schooling, etc. The typical home buyer searches for months online before making a decision so you are not alone. In addition, the typical home buyer searches for larger homes with far more amenities that they can realistically afford because at this point it's a fantasy and, let's face it, fantasy is fun. This is a huge financial decision with many ramifications so a little prudence is in order.

Where should you search for a home online? There are a multitude of websites dedicated to Real Estate that are sponsored by organizations, companies and individuals. For homes in Contra Costa County, California, I recommend my professional website, www.dancraddock.com, where you can search the Multiple Listing Service (MLS), sign up to receive notifications when new homes that match your criteria come on the market. You can also find great articles about current market conditions, fixing up a home, inspections and a lot more. Other top real estate websites include the National Realtor Association; www.realtor.com, Trulia; www.trulia.com, Zillow; www.zillow.com and my broker's website www.resolutere.com. In addition, there are many great Realtor websites that specialize in just about every city and county in the United States.

There a lot of people throughout the country that use Zillow and love it. Beware of the information though. I recently had a client that saw a home that sold for over $400,000 listed on Zillow with a sales price of just over $13,000. Zillow provides what they call a 'zestimate' which is Zillow's estimated value of the home. These 'zestimates' are not always accurate and it's best to get the information from a Realtor who will provide, at no cost to you, a Comparable Market Analysis (CMA). This CMA will contain pricing information on homes that have recently sold, those that are pending or that have a contract on them and those that are still on the market.

Up to this point, you're in fantasy land because you really don't know whether you can actually afford a home or specifically how much of a home you can afford.

The first thing you'll need to do is determine if you are qualified to purchase a home and if so, how much you can afford to spend on a house. Before you can write a contract to purchase a home, you will need to be pre-approved for a loan. Once you have received a written pre-approval letter you can move on to the next step which is finding a Realtor to help you with your purchase.

Why should I get pre-approved and not just pre-qualified? What is the difference? Pre-qualification often takes just a few minutes and most lenders will provide this service at no cost to you. However, a pre-qualification letter is non-binding and is frankly not worth the paper it is written on. With a pre-qualification, the lender has not acquired enough information from you and more importantly has not verified your financial information in order to make a proper assessment of your financial position.

The pre-approval process involves your lender actually verifying your assets, debts and credit history. After they verify this information and make a determination that you qualify for a mortgage, they will issue a letter stating that you are pre-approved for a loan of a certain amount that is good for a specified amount of time, usually 3 months. While some lenders will charge a fee for this service, most will not because they want your business.

Before you can get a pre-approval letter, you'll need to gather certain documents together. If you are financing the home with another person, such as your spouse, you'll need the information for both borrowers. Being prepared for your visit will impress the mortgage broker or banker. If you work for someone else, as opposed to being self-employed, you will need to get the following together:

1. Last year's tax return
2. Last two months of paystubs
3. Last two months of bank statements

The following are some questions that the lender will ask you:

- Employment and income

  Where do you work? How long have you worked there? What is your annual income? Is your income derived from a salary, commission, bonuses or a combination? Is your income stable? Who was your previous employer? Do you receive child support? Do you pay child support? What is the source of any other income you receive?

- Liabilities

  What are your current debts? What is the minimum payment for each of your long term debts? How much have you been paying each month on these debts? Of your debts, how much is owed on credit cards and auto loans?

- Assets

  What assets do you have? What is the current balance of each? Where will the money come from for your down payment and closing costs?

- Credit

  Instead of the lender asking you questions about your credit, the lender will pull your credit report from at least one of three credit bureaus. If you have any negative items on your credit report, the lender will certainly ask you about them. If the negative items have been reported incorrectly, the lender should be able to tell you how to get the items removed or at least suspended until they can be further reviewed.

If you are self-employed then you'll need the above information plus your last year's business tax return if you have one. Being self-employed is a little different than having a job and it takes a little more effort for the lender to determine how much money you'll be pre-approved for.

Where do I get a pre-approval letter? Well, you have two choices. The first is to go to your bank or credit union and speak with a loan officer. Banks can be a great choice if you have impeccable credit, a long history of employment and a long history with the particular bank or credit union. Credit Unions, while typically not known for their mortgage lending, can be competitive alternatives to banks by offering lower closing costs and mortgage interest rates. The second choice is to find a good mortgage broker either locally or online. Mortgage brokers have access to many different lending sources of money (sometimes over a hundred) whereas bankers only have access to their own bank's funds. Because of the number of lending options available, using a mortgage broker may be the easiest solution for most borrowers.

Mortgage brokers are easy to find and, with the new regulations instituted after the housing crisis, they are more regulated. You should be comfortable with your mortgage broker as they can make or break your deal. Here are ten questions to ask a mortgage broker. If you don't receive the answers you like, move on to another mortgage broker.

1. <u>Which type of loan is best for me?</u> – Reputable lenders will find out more about your particular situation before giving you options. They will also explain the differences between FHA, conventional loans and if you are a veteran, VA loans. More people are purchasing homes with FHA loans than ever before because of the low down payment requirement, typically between 3.5% and 5%. There are loan amount limitations with a FHA loan but they are usually high enough to allow borrowers to purchase an average priced single

family home in most parts of the country.

2. <u>Should I get a fixed or adjustable rate loan and what are the interest rates and annual percentage rates?</u> – The mortgage broker should ask you questions about your particular situation and then give you the best options and rates.

3. <u>What are the discount points and origination fees?</u> – Each point is equal to 1% of the loan amount. The mortgage broker should talk to you about the option to buy down the interest rate by paying points at the time your loan closes. In addition, some lenders charge an origination fee to process your loan.

4. <u>What are all the costs involved?</u> – It's very important to know upfront what all the costs are so that you can compare different options.

5. <u>Will the Lender guarantee the Good Faith Estimate (GFE)?</u> – The GFE is a breakdown of all the costs associated with your loan. In has been the practice of some lenders to inflate the GFE to include fluctuations that might occur. In the past, some lenders were known to provide a low ball estimate just to get

your business but this practice is largely gone due to the new regulations put into place.

6. <u>Do you offer Loan Rate locks?</u> – Most lenders allow you to lock in a rate for 45 to 60 days to protect you from interest rate increases. Longer rate-lock periods may be available for an additional fee.

7. <u>Is there a Prepayment Penalty?</u> – This is extremely important. Some lenders charge a fee if you pay off (prepay) the loan in the first 5 years. So, if you wish to sell the home, pay off the loan or refinance during this period, you'll have to pay a penalty which can be substantial. Always get a loan with no prepayment penalty.

8. <u>Are you equipped to approve loans in-house?</u> – This is neither a good nor a bad thing but it gives you an indication of the length of time it will take the lender to make a decision on your loan. If they can approve loans in-house then you likely can get a quicker approval. In addition, if you have a history with the bank that approves loans in-house, they may be more apt to approve your loan even if your situation is borderline.

9. <u>How much time do you need to fund?</u> – The average loan processing time is between 21 and 45 days. Make sure you ask the following:
   a. What is the anticipated turnaround time?
   b. What obstacles could possibly hold up the closing?
   c. How long after the final application approval will the loan fund?

10. <u>How many lenders does the mortgage broker work with and are they approved for FHA financing?</u> – Since the housing crisis, FHA loans have become very popular because they are government backed and require the least amount of down payment.

The banker or mortgage broker is an extremely important piece in the process so make sure that you are comfortable and confident that they can produce for you. Once you get a contract approved, you'll be relying on your banker or mortgage broker to come through with your loan approval which can make or break the deal you have worked out with the seller.

After obtaining pre-approval, your mortgage broker or banker should tell you the following basic do's and don'ts:

1. DO pay all your payments on time.
2. DO make sure that you have the down payment and closing cost money.
3. DON'T open any new charge or installment accounts.
4. DON'T buy a new car or truck.
5. DON'T charge anything else on your credit cards like furniture, etc. until you have the keys in your hands.
6. DON'T be late on any of your payments.
7. DON'T loan money to anyone else or co-sign for anyone else.
8. DON'T change jobs

CHAPTER 4

CHOOSING A REALTOR

"If you think hiring a professional is expensive,
wait till you hire an amateur"   **- Red Adair**

First of all, I'd like to set the record straight on the definition of a Realtor versus a Real Estate Agent. A Realtor is a Real Estate Agent that is a member of the National Association of Realtors. Only about half of the Real Estate licensees are Realtors. Realtors belong to a nationwide organization that stands behind them providing information that is not available to non-Realtors. In this book, I will be using the term Realtor whenever I refer to a Real Estate Agent but you now know the difference.

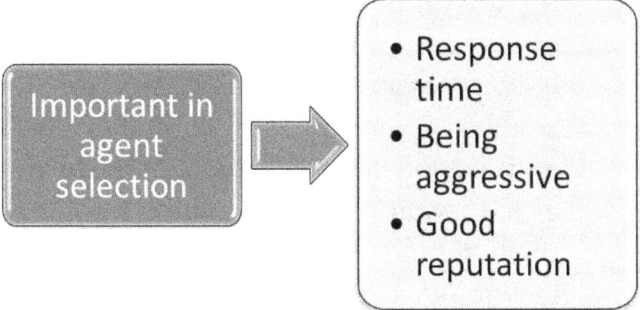

Important in agent selection → • Response time • Being aggressive • Good reputation

Choosing a Realtor can be a very stressful ordeal or it can be very easy. By the end of this chapter you'll be comfortable with making the decision as to which Realtor to partner with. Most people have a friend, neighbor or co-worker that knows a Realtor that they can recommend to you. In fact, in southwest Florida, there are more Realtors per capita than anywhere else in the country.

Some people choose a house first and then call the Realtor representing the seller (the Listing Agent) who they end up working with. This is not the smart thing to do. A Listing Agent has certain responsibilities towards the Seller so they are working on the Sellers behalf and not yours. Yes, they can surely assist you in purchasing a home but their allegiance is with a Seller and the consequences could be very costly. You need a Realtor that is working for you and looking out for your interests.

At a minimum, the Realtor you choose should be licensed in the state in which they work as a broker or an agent. The Realtor should be experienced and working full time as a Realtor having worked in the industry for at least a couple of years. They should be personable and a good listener who is able to determine exactly what you are searching for. In addition, they should be technologically savvy since technology is so much a part of our daily life.

The following are the basic duties that all Realtors have. Depending on the type of representation or agency, other duties may be added.

1) To put the client's interests above anyone else's
2) Keep the client's information confidential
3) Obey the client's lawful instructions
4) Report to the client anything that would be useful
5) Account to the client for any money involved

Realtors are paid by commission from the seller of the home. In other words, as a buyer, you get a licensed Realtor for FREE. A Realtor that works with buyers is called a Buyer's Agent. Make sure that your Realtor has a Buyers Agreement outlining the benefits of working with this Realtor. Being a Buyer's agent is a tough job because you can fire your agent. Just remember that a Buyer's agent that agrees to work with you incurs actual out-of-pocket costs for gasoline, wear and tear on their automobile, office supplies and often times meals so it's a big deal to them if they get fired.

When choosing a Realtor you should interview them at their office first. You need to see where they work, the support system in the office and whether the office is professional or not. In addition, you also need to meet the Broker (usually the Owner of the Real Estate firm) so you know who stands behind the Realtor you are considering.

Compile a list of questions to ask the Realtor. If you don't get the answers or explanations that you require then go to another Realtor. Remember, this is a large transaction so you want a Realtor that you can feel comfortable working with and one with your interests at heart. The Realtor profession is made up of all types of Realtors and some will not be compatible with you. You'll find agents that have a minimum commission amount. These agents will not take on a buyer that wants to purchase a property below a given amount or they will ask you to pay the difference between their minimum commission and the commission earned on the sale. Depending on the agent, this may or may not be something that you want to consider. You'll also come across agents that will tell you up front that they are not compatible with you and will suggest another agent for you to work with.

Choose an agent that:

1. Will listen to your needs
2. Will take the time to explain things you might not understand
3. Will work on your time schedule – If you only have nights off or can only look on certain days of the week or weekend then pick someone that will cater to you.
4. Has an extended team of mortgage brokers, inspectors, attorney's, etc. that they have worked with and can refer to you.
5. Will show you homes based on your criteria not based on the commission the seller is paying.
6. Will provide timely communication and in the manner that you prescribe whether it be email, text, phone or in person.
7. Has great negotiation skills
8. Knows the current market.
9. Will have you sign a Buyers Agreement outlining the benefits of working with them.

Ideally, you'll want an agent that is HUNGRY. An agent that will do whatever they can to find your dream home. You should feel like you are their most important client at all times.

By default, a Realtor in Florida works as a Transaction Broker which is unlike most of the states. A Transaction Broker doesn't actually work for you but will assist you with the transaction. I know this is a difficult concept to grasp and one that most people don't even know about. In order to get a Realtor to work solely for you then you'll need to have them transition from a Transaction Broker to a Buyer's Agent. If you are unsure if your Realtor is acting as a Transaction Broker or a Buyer's Agent, simply ask them.

Finally, in most states, you'll need to sign an agency agreement with the Realtor that spells out the responsibilities of the Realtor.

CHAPTER 5

WHAT TYPE OF LOAN SHOULD I GET?

"Each problem that I solved became a rule which served afterwards to solve other problems." - **Rene Descartes**

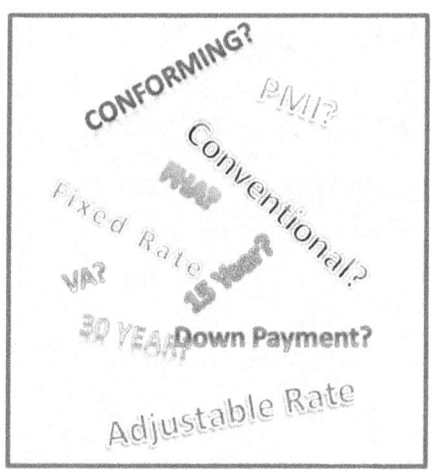

Determining which type of loan is best for you can be a daunting task, but it doesn't have to be. Once you know the common terms and nomenclature, you should have no problem deciding which type of loan to get from your Banker or Mortgage Broker.

One of the things to consider is how long you plan to own the home. If you plan to be in your home for five years or less then it makes sense to get a loan with the lowest possible monthly payments in the first five years. If you plan to stay in your home for more than five years then it makes sense to get a loan with constant monthly payments for the life of the loan. If you don't know how long you plan on staying in your home then I suggest that you be conservative and assume that you'll stay in your home for more than 5 years. As of 2011, the average American was living in their home for nine years.

I will detail all the types of loans that are available and provide you with enough information so that you can ask intelligent questions of your Banker or Loan Broker, who is responsible for helping you choose the type of loan that is right for you. There are so many loan programs available today that trying to select the right one for you may seem overwhelming. However, armed with the basic information in this chapter, you will be able to understand how the most popular loan programs work and to identify which loan characteristics are most important to you.

Mortgage lenders are typically banks, credit unions and mortgage brokers. As you might have guessed, these entities don't have an unlimited amount of money to lend. As a result, they have to sell loans on the backend so they can replenish their money in order to make more loans.

Most of these loans are sold to the Government Sponsored Enterprises (GSE) such as Fannie Mae, financial institutions, insurance companies and pension funds. This means that the company you originally get your loan from may not be the same company who owns your loan and is collecting your payments six months down the road. In fact, your loan may be "sold" to several different investors over its lifetime. This is common practice in the industry and should not cause you any concern. Just be sure you keep your eyes open for notifications from your lender about where your payments are to be sent as the payment address will usually change each time your loan is sold to a new investor.

I suggest that you not set up an automatic payment via your bank or credit union for your mortgage payment. When your loan gets sold, if you don't change the routing of your automatic payment as per the new lender, your payment may go to the wrong lender. It's very, very difficult to get that money back. In the meantime, you'll have to make the payment to the new lender while you're trying to get the money back from the old lender so you don't affect your credit score. It has happened to many people including me.

A mortgage broker might have a list of 100 different loan programs that offer various terms. The most popular loan has a 30 year term. A 15 year term is also quite popular, but it involves a higher monthly payment since you're paying the loan back in half the time. There are also 40 and 50 year loans, but these are specialty products that are used in situations where the borrower cannot afford payments on a 30 year mortgage. I would not recommend these products as anything but a last resort since you end up paying an enormous amount of interest over the course of the loan.

No matter which loan program you choose, keep in mind that mortgage loans are set up so that most of your monthly payment in the early years of the loan goes towards interest and only a small amount goes to reduce the principle balance. As the loan progresses in its later years, most of your monthly payment goes towards the principle and less towards the interest.

You might have heard the term 'amortization'. This refers to the paying off of a debt in regular installments over a period of time. A 30 year loan is amortized over 30 years whereas a 15 year loan is amortized over 15 years.

Now let's move onto loan types. There are basically two types of loans that you can get:

- Fixed rate
- Adjustable rate

A <u>fixed rate loan</u> has an interest rate that does not change for the entire term of the loan which means that your monthly payments will remain the same. If your monthly payment in the first month is $1,000 then your monthly payment will continue to be $1,000 over the life of the loan.

With an <u>adjustable rate loan</u>, the interest rate fluctuates according to a certain schedule either monthly, semi-annually, annually or other time period as designated by the lender. If the interest rate on your loan goes up or down, your payment will also increase or decrease. This means that the amount of your first payment may not be the same amount as subsequent payments. In addition, adjustable rate loans sometimes come with a balloon payment. A balloon payment is an unusually large payment consisting of the actual principal balance due at a specified point in a loan.

For example, if your loan has a balloon payment in five years, you will have a choice to make before that deadline. Either you pay the entire balance that is due on the loan, which is normally impossible to do, or you refinance the loan. By refinancing the loan, you are actually making that huge payment but it's coming out of the lending institutions pocket.

Adjustable rate loans usually come with a periodic and a lifetime cap, or ceiling, which is the maximum amount that the interest rate on that the loan change during the specified period. For example, let's say that you have a loan that is scheduled to adjust once per year with an initial rate of 3.5%, with a periodic cap of 2.0% and a lifetime cap of 10.0%. This means that the interest rate can only increase or decrease by a maximum of 2.0% each year and cannot go any higher than 10.0% during the life of the loan. In addition, these loans usually come with a floor, which is the minimum interest rate that will be charged during the life of the loan. When interest rates are low, adjustable rate loans are not really feasible in most cases but your Mortgage broker or Banker can explain this all for you.

Let's move on to loan classifications. Loans are classified based upon the different characteristics they have, such as loan amount, loan-to-value, etc. Below are some classifications that are common in the industry.

<u>Conforming Loans and Non-Conforming Loans</u>

Conforming loans are those that meet all the underwriting requirements, such as debt-to-income ratio and documentation guidelines, set forth by the Government Sponsored Enterprises, Fannie Mae and Freddie Mac. Every lender basically uses the same guidelines so the real determination as to whether a loan is a conforming or non-conforming loan is the loan amount. The conforming loan amount limit is currently $417,000 in most of the country. In states with higher priced real estate like California, the conforming loan limits are higher. In Contra Costa County California, the conforming loan limit is currently $625,500 but this limit is subject to change annually.

Fannie Mae, Federal National Mortgage Association, is a corporation created by the Federal Government that buys and sells conventional mortgages. In addition, they set the maximum loan amount and requirements for borrowers.

Conventional Loans

Conventional mortgage loans are the most common type of loan but require a higher down payment than an FHA loan. These loans are not insured by any of the GSE's. They do follow the loan limits set by Fannie Mae and Freddie Mac. Nonconforming loans that don't meet the GSE requirements are also considered conventional loans. Your Banker or Mortgage

Broker will be able to elaborate on the characteristics of these loans.

FHA Loans

FHA loans have increased in popularity since the economic downturn. These loans are guaranteed by the government which reduces the risk for the lender but are subject to the lender's rules for credit scores, debt-to-income ratio, etc. The borrower might meet the minimum FHA standards but may not meet the lender's additional requirements which will result in a denial of the loan. Most lenders have a minimum credit score requirement of 620 which is currently higher than the FHA minimum score.

If you don't have a lot of money for a down payment then an FHA loan might be your best choice since the minimum down payment is as low as 3.5% of the contract sales price of the home.

VA Loans

The VA loan program was established by the United States Department of Veterans Affairs to assist veterans and their families in obtaining financing for a home. The

Department of Veterans Affairs does not directly offer the loans but instead they establish the rules for those that qualify, dictate the specific terms of the loan and insure the loan against default. The VA offers 100% financing based on the value of the home.

If you are in the military or are retired from the military then a VA loan might be your best option. In order to be eligible, you must present a certificate of eligibility which establishes your record of military service with the lender.

Having said all this, the real question is whether you want a fixed or adjustable rate mortgage. All the other questions will be answered by how much of a down payment you can afford.

CHAPTER 6

WHAT IS PMI AND DO I NEED IT?

"Nothing in the world is more dangerous than sincere ignorance and conscientious stupidity."
- Martin Luther King Jr.

PMI stands for Private Mortgage Insurance and is typically required lenders to offset the risk of providing a loan to you with a low down payment. Whether you need it or not depends on how much money you are putting down on the new home.

If your down payment is less than 20% of the appraised value or sale price of the home, you may be required to obtain PMI by your lender. The monthly premium is from .5% to 1% of the principle of the loan per year. The premiums can be paid monthly (along with your monthly mortgage payment), annually or in a single lump sum at the time the loan closes.

For example, if your loan is $200,000, and your PMI is .5% then your monthly PMI payment is (.005 x 200,000)/12 = $83.33.

There are a couple of ways to avoid paying the monthly PMI payment:

Pay a Higher Interest Rate – Some lenders will waive the mortgage insurance requirement if the buyer agrees to accept a higher mortgage interest rate. This rate will generally be .75% to 1% higher depending on your down payment. The advantage of this option is that mortgage interest is currently tax deductible. There are income phase outs on mortgage interest tax deductions. You will need to check with your tax professional to see if it is more advantageous to go with a higher interest rate or to pay the monthly PMI payment.

Use an 80-10-10 Loan – This consists of a primary or first mortgage loan of 80%, a second mortgage loan of 10% and a down payment of 10%, thus the name 80-10-10. Since PMI is only charged on first mortgage loans that have a loan-to-value in excess of 80%, you avoid the requirement by financing 10% of your purchase price into a second mortgage loan. The disadvantage of this option is that second mortgage loans normally charge a higher interest rate than a first mortgage loan, so the total of your monthly payments will be higher than having only e first mortgage loan at 80%. But, keep in mind that the interest you pay on the second mortgage loan may be tax deductible.

CHAPTER 7

SHOULD I PURCHASE A PREVIOUSLY OWNED HOME OR NEW CONSTRUCTION?

Owning a home is the culmination of many years of hard work and the realization of the American Dream. ~ ***Solomon Ortiz***

Most people just gravitate toward buying a previously owned home because that is what is most available in the area and/or probably what they are used to i.e. comfort zone. My first home was a new tri-level home in Georgia which we only lived in for six months due to a job transfer. It was a home that someone else had purchased but the contract fell through so all the options were already picked out but we were the first occupants. Throughout my life my parents had purchased previously owned homes but I thought I'd do something different. As a matter of fact, most of the homes I've purchased for my primary residence have been new homes with one being a custom built home including ownership in part of a lake. I guess I got the bug. My suggestion is to search out new construction if it is available in your area and at least go and see what is available and what amenities are included in the price. According to my wife, another good reason to view model homes is to get decorating tips.

Depending on where you intend to live, you might not have a choice between buying a previously owned home or building a brand new one. In some areas of the country, there is little to no available land to build new homes. In these areas, if you want to build a new house, you must first tear down an existing home.

Some of the advantages of buying a previously owned home are:

- The yard is already in and hopefully has matured.
- All of the "new home issues", such as faulty appliances, leaking roofs, cracked tiles, etc. might have been addressed.
- You can easily assess your neighbors and the neighborhood.

- It's easier to visualize living there.
- You know exactly what you are getting.
- There are no construction delays or increased cost of materials.
- You don't have to spend additional money for upgrades.
- The house has settled so any issues associated with settling like foundation cracks or cracks in the walls are usually taken care of.
- You can usually get into the home in 45 days or less rather than waiting months for a home to be built.
- The price is usually cheaper than new construction when you factor in the additional costs for the yard as well as upgrades.

Buying new construction is quite a bit different than purchasing a previously owned home. For one thing, it is definitely more stressful as you not only have to decide on which subdivision but which builder, which particular model, which lot, what interior/exterior paint colors, what upgrades you want but you have to deal with all the added expenses you'll incur once you gain possession of the home. In addition, it is a time consuming adventure which will require flexibility on your part. Even though it is a new home, there will be issues that will need to be resolved. Most of these issues will be covered under your new homeowner's warranty but, nevertheless, they still need to be addressed which will take up your time.

There are basically two ways to buy new construction:

1. Build a Custom Home

Custom built homes are just that – customized to your own liking. There are many ways to have a custom home built from finding an architect to finding a builder and selecting your own lot and plans to starting with a spec home and customizing it to fit your needs. Most often, the only pictures you have of the finished home are the building plans and the artist's drawings. Most people have a hard time visualizing what the customized home will ultimately look like, so this can be a very stressful undertaking. However, if you have the funds, have the time and want to truly create your own environment then I strongly recommend building a custom home.

Be advised that, in the end, it will cost more than you think it will, it will take longer to build than you think it will and the preparation time will be longer. Make sure that you solicit the assistance of a good real estate Attorney and thoroughly research the architect and/or builder you are considering. I have friends that lost a lot of money when their builder went bankrupt before the construction of their new home was completed. Another good piece of advice is to talk to others that have recently built a new home in the area you are looking in. You might gain some helpful tips that can save you big money.

2. **Buy in a Subdivision**

Buying new construction in a subdivision might be the best route to take over a custom built home if this is your first foray into new home construction. It is definitely less stressful than building a custom home and there are many advantages like:

- You don't have to search for an architect and a builder.
- You are given a range of lots to choose from, which alleviates the need to find and purchase your own lot.
- The subdivisions usually have model homes that are usually decorated to the hilt with many of the options that are available.
- You can make frequent trips to the model homes to take pictures,

measure for furniture and visualize all of your things in the home. Don't underestimate how big of a morale booster it can be to have access to a model of your future home and it will make the time go by faster.

Since there are so many facets to buying new construction, the builders really have it down to a science. They have a plan for you to follow along with a timeline, making the process seem easy and straightforward. On the other hand, the builder's contract that you will be considerably longer than a standard Realtor's contract so you'll want to pay close attention to the details. The builder will also require your signature on many forms that are builder specific. Read all of the documents thoroughly and consult with your Realtor or an attorney if you do not understand any of the language before signing them.

In addition, many builders strongly suggest that you use their preferred lender and will require you to pay a larger deposit for any upgrades that you choose if you elect to go with a different lender. They do this in case your financing falls through and you can't complete the purchase of the home. This may result in the builder having to sell the home with upgrades that may not be what the majority of buyers are looking for resulting in a lower sales price or a longer time on the market. Everyone's tastes are different so keep this in mind when you are matching colors and patterns.

It behooves you to have your own representation when purchasing a new construction home, whether it be custom built or a spec home in a subdivision. A Realtor can guide you through the process, look out for your interests and recommend other professionals that may be required during the buying process. Having your own Realtor costs you nothing yet gives you piece of mind and will keep you clear of pitfalls which may result in financial penalties. Yes, there are penalties for not following the builder's schedule. Contractually, the builder has the ability to delay the transaction, but you usually cannot do so without paying a hefty penalty for each day that the closing is delayed.

REMEMBER, before you get into a car and head on over to the new subdivisions, contact your Realtor first and have them meet you there so they can be registered as your Realtor. If you tour a new subdivision for the first time without a Realtor then most builders will not recognize the Realtor as your representative, which means they will not be able to assist you in your dealings with the builder. A good

Realtor will be more than happy to meet you to preview a new development and tour model homes and available lots. If you find a Realtor that won't, I'll be glad to do it or recommend a Realtor in your area that will be glad to accompany you.

CHAPTER 8

THE BUYING PROCESS

"The best investment on Earth is earth."
-Louis Glickman, American business
executive

Now that you've chosen your Realtor, been pre-approved for your mortgage loan and are ready to start looking at homes to purchase, the next step is the buying process. Your Realtor should advise you of the process and help you at every step along the way. This chapter is meant to inform you of the many steps along the way once you have found your ideal home.

Buying Process Chart

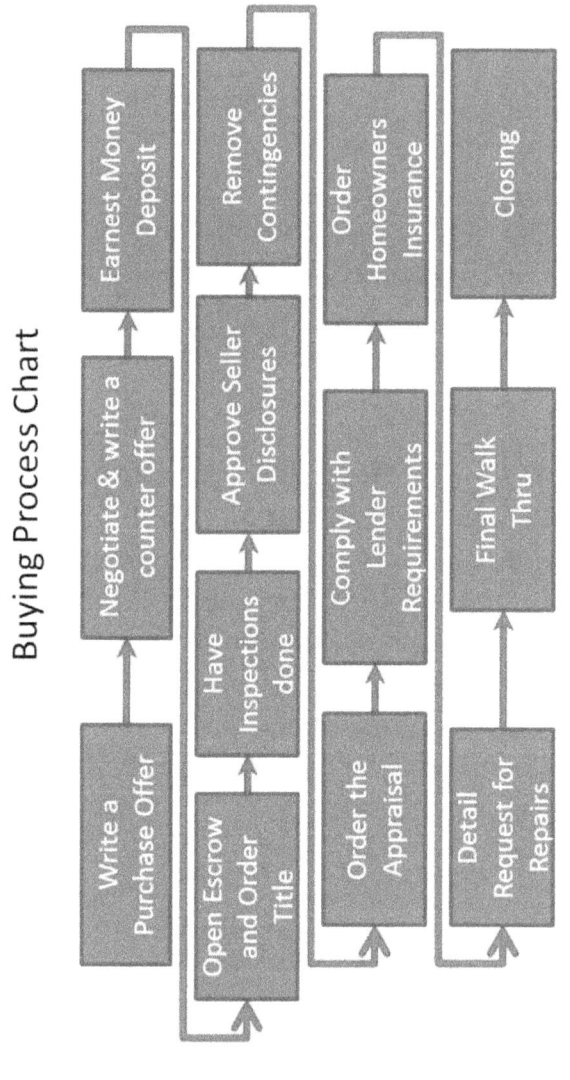

Write a Purchase Offer	→	Negotiate & write a counter offer	→	Earnest Money Deposit
Open Escrow and Order Title	→	Have Inspections done	→	Approve Seller Disclosures	→	Remove Contingencies
Order the Appraisal	→	Comply with Lender Requirements	→	Order Homeowners Insurance
Detail Request for Repairs	→	Final Walk Thru	→	Closing

Step 1: Write a Purchase Offer

Depending on what state you live in, there might be two types of contracts that you can use to present an offer – the AS IS contract and the Purchase or Sale contract. There are times when the type of contract is dictated by the seller and other times when you can choose either one. Have your Realtor explain the advantages and disadvantages of each contract to you. In California, there is only one type of contract that Realtor's use which is the Purchase or Sale Contract.

Again, your Realtor will give you advice on how much to offer depending on the particular market that you are in – either a buyer's or seller's market. In a buyer's market, there is usually a large inventory of homes on the market and prices are usually in a downward trend. A buyer's market means that your offer should be considerably less than it would be in a seller's market. By contrast, in a seller's market, there is a shortage of homes and prices are generally going up. It is not uncommon in a seller's market to receive multiple offers for more than the asking price thus starting a bidding war.

Your first offer is extremely important. It tells the seller if you are really interested in their home rather than just looking to find a deal somewhere. Make sure that you have your Realtor do a Comparable Market Analysis (CMA) so that you know exactly what has sold in the area and for what price. Given the type of market that you are in coupled with the knowledge from the CMA and the particulars of the home (square footage, number of bedrooms, etc.) that you are wanting to purchase, you will be able to make an offer that is both fair and acceptable to the seller.

Depending upon the market, lowball offers, offers well below the asking price, may be acceptable. The risk you take is that the seller is offended and they refuse to provide a counter offer. So, before making a deeply discounted offer to the seller, seek the advice of your Realtor, who can help you come up with an offer that will have the best chance of being accepted by the seller.

Your offer will include an offer acceptance date and a closing date among a host of other information. It is important to have a short acceptance date i.e. 24 hours or so. This has a dual purpose: it tells the seller that you mean business and also that you want the least number of competing offers during that time. The closing date is also very important. The shorter the time to close, the better your deal looks to the seller. All cash deals usually have a 2 week closing date which appeals to most sellers. Those buyers having to get a loan cannot compete with 2 weeks but they can possibly do less than 4 weeks but only with agreement with your Banker or Mortgage Broker. Get specific advice from your Realtor based on your particular situation and location.

Generally, everything that is permanently affixed to the walls of the home are included in the deal, but it doesn't hurt to detail on the contract any items that you specifically want to make sure that you get. It doesn't hurt to ask for more than you want in order to create a negotiating platform. Again, depending on the type of market this may be a good strategy or it may be a bad one. Ask your Realtor.

Cash is KING. The more cash you have, the better your chance of getting the deal. However, if you don't have a lot of cash, there are still ways to get your offer at the top of the stack even above an all cash offer. Sellers definitely look at the deal logically; however, there is also an emotional component that most often is not exploited. By appealing to the emotions of the seller, you can thwart logic. Your Realtor should be able to fill in all the details.

Step 2: Negotiate and Write a Counter Offer

Once you have submitted your offer, the seller has the option of accepting your offer, providing a counter offer or doing nothing. Should the seller offer a counter to your offer, it's up to you to decide whether to accept the counter or offer another counter or cancel the negotiations. This can be very tricky so you'll need to rely on your Realtor's negotiation skills and experience to guide you. Having your Realtor relay personal family details to the seller or seller's Realtor can also have an effect on whether the seller will take your deal or not.

There is one critical thing to keep in mind during the process: once the seller has submitted a counter offer, your original offer is GONE. That's right, at this point, the only offer on the table is the counter offer submitted by the seller. The tables have turned and the seller is now in the driver's seat. You don't have another offer outstanding until you submit a counter and it is delivered and accepted by the seller.

During the counter offer phase, the seller can receive and accept another offer even though they have sent you a counter offer. This might not seem fair but that is how it works. This is why when you get into the negotiation stage it is critical that you are available to accept or counter as quickly as possible. On a counter offer, make sure that you initial the changes and put the time and date because time is of the essence in a real estate purchase negotiation.

Step 3: Earnest Money Deposit

This step actually goes along with Step 1 as you cannot have a valid contract without consideration. The consideration is the escrow deposit or earnest money. The escrow deposit is usually held by a Title Company or an Attorney in a non-interest bearing account. Earnest money could also be held by a Real Estate Brokerage Company in the same type of account but, due to the many liability concerns associated with escrow deposits, it is usually left up to the Title Company or Attorney.

The amount of the escrow deposit depends on the market and the price of the home. At a minimum it can be as little as $500 and can be upwards of $25,000 or more. The escrow deposit is the first indication to the seller of how serious you are as a buyer. The more money you put up, the more serious you appear to the seller. It is not unheard of for two identical offers to come in and the seller chooses the one with the higher escrow deposit. At this point, the seller doesn't know much about the buyer except that one offer stands out because of a larger escrow deposit. If you are not going with a VA loan then you will have to make a down payment of at least 3.5% with an FHA loan and at least 20% of the purchase price with a conventional loan. Knowing this, a large escrow deposit that approaches your required down payment amount may make your offer stand out from any others while keeping your financial exposure the same.

The big question about an escrow deposit is: is it refundable? If the deal goes south, can I get my money back? The answer is it depends. If the contract is not accepted by the seller then it is definitely refundable. In other situations it depends on what the contract says and which type of contract you use. Have your Realtor explain all the ramifications to you based on the type of contract that you are submitting.

Step 4: Open Escrow and Order Title

When the seller's representative has taken the escrow deposit, they have a certain number of days to deposit the check or to give the check into an escrow account or give the check to the Title Company or Attorney, depending upon the particular laws of that state. Once the Title Company or Attorney has an executed contract and the escrow deposit, they will then follow the mandate in the contract as to when they will start working on the Title policy. The Title Company or Attorney will provide the Realtor with the escrow officer's name; phone number and escrow file number which you'll need to give to your lender and insurance company. Escrow is an extremely important part of the process which I will outline in the next chapter.

Step 5: Have a Home Inspection and any other Inspections Done

It is essential that you have a home inspection performed by a qualified inspector during the inspection period provided for in the sales contract. A home inspection will let you know what is wrong with the home. Minor problems are expected and even welcomed as they can be used to negotiate other concessions from the seller. The main reason for the home inspection is to find any major structural problems. If the home inspector finds structural problems with the home then you should consult with your Realtor before continuing with the purchase. In most cases, structural problems will mean that you should cancel the contract and find another home.

Make sure that you are present for the home inspection and choose an inspector that will let you follow him/her around and ask questions. You might want to film the inspection as you will find out so many things about your home that you probably won't remember. Having a video to refer back to later will also give you a baseline if you should have problems with the home in the future.

Step 6: Approve any Seller Disclosures

The seller disclosure is a document that the seller is required to present to the prospective buyer. The document usually contains a series of questions related to the condition of key aspects of the home. With foreclosures, the lending institution usually has not seen the house and has no knowledge of the condition of the home so the disclosure is merely a formality. In California, the Listing Realtor is required to provide an Agent Visual Inspection (AVID) Document, which lists any items that the Realtor might have noticed as they performed a visual inspection of the property. Realtors are not qualified inspectors but, items noted on the AVID are issues that you should bring up to your inspector.

Step 7: Remove Contingencies

Contingencies are conditions that you have placed in the contract and addendums that need to be completed before you can close on the home. An example is a financing contingency. Once you have obtained a formal loan approval then this contingency should be removed by the lender. Additional contingencies might be a home, pest or roof inspection or certain repairs required on the property.   Usually written notice of the contingency removal is required or the closing will not proceed.

Step 8: Order the Appraisal

Your loan officer will be the one that orders the appraisal which can cost $250 or more. This fee is normally paid by the buyer as part of the closing costs or directly to the appraiser upon completion of the work.

Step 9: Comply with your Lenders Requirements

Lenders will often require you to answer questions about anomalies on your credit report, lapses in your employment, strange deposits to your accounts and any other issues that might be considered out of the ordinary. There are very few buyers that have a perfect history so lenders will usually come up with something, however trivial it might be.

Step 10: Order your Homeowner's Insurance Policy

Your Realtor should refer you to several insurance companies or insurance brokers that you can contact to purchase your homeowners insurance. Usually, you will need to purchase a one year paid up insurance policy before the lender will agree to fund the loan. This can paid directly to the insurer or through the escrow at closing depending upon the requirements of your particular state.

Step 11: Detail the Request for Repairs

If you are using an AS IS Contract then any repairs are your responsibility. If you are using a Purchase and Sale Contract, there are provisions in the contract for repairs. These repairs should be discussed with your Realtor. Major repairs should be negotiated and depending upon the offer, the seller may be willing to pay for them or at least share in their cost. This will vary depending on the type of market that you're in so seek guidance from your Realtor.

Step 12: Do the Final Walk Through

On the night before or the day of closing, you should do a final walk through with your Realtor. The purpose of the walk through is to make sure that the house is in the same condition as it was when you signed the contract. If things have changed, such as vandalism, theft, water or other damage, you should request the guidance of your Realtor to determine the next course of action. It might be just a matter of delaying the closing until the house is back to the same condition when you contracted for it. An alternative is for the closing to proceed on schedule having the closing attorney or Title agent hold some of the proceeds to the seller in the escrow account until the house is in an acceptable condition. If the damage is such that the house will not be acceptable for a prolonged period of time then cancellation of the contract may be the best course of action. Make sure you check with your Realtor, your Attorney or your Title agent for any consequences that might result from any action you are considering.

Step 13: The Closing

Congratulations! You've finally made it to the closing. Everything is done and you are ready to make the home your own. The closing is made up of two distinct parts. The first part consists of signing all the papers and the second part is the transfer of funds from your lender into the escrow account to complete the transaction (funds must be in the form of a certified or cashier's check or bank wire). The closing can take place in stages as the seller usually signs the papers first before the buyer. Funds will be transferred on the day of closing or the following morning. Also, during the closing, you will also receive the keys, garage door openers, alarm codes, etc. to the home.

If either the buyer or seller is not able to attend the closing then the closing agent or attorney will do what is called a 'Mail Away'. The documents are prepared by the attorney or Title Company and sent via overnight mail to the out of town party with directions as to where to sign. The Mail Away envelope will contain an overnight envelope to send the signed documents back to the attorney or Title Company.

Now that you've completed the closing and have the keys to your new home, you have one very important thing to do before moving in. The first thing you should do is to change or rekey the locks, recode the garage door openers and change the alarm codes. Making these changes will ensure that your new home is secure from anyone with prior access. This particular step is vital but sometimes forgotten.

CHAPTER 9

THE ESCROW PROCESS

"Every person who invests in well-selected real estate in a growing section of a prosperous community adopts the surest and safest method of becoming independent, for real estate is the basis of wealth."

-Theodore Roosevelt

As I said previously, the escrow process is an extremely important part of the home buying process. In fact, it is the backbone of the entire process. The process begins when you have an accepted signed contract and remains active until the deal closes, the deed is recorded and all the funds have been transferred. In some cases, escrow may remain open after closing due to provisions in the contract such as a rent back agreement.

The responsibility for the escrow process is either the Title Company or Closing Attorney depending on the particular laws in your state. Check with your Realtor for more information.

The following process chart detailing the escrow process is provided by Fidelity National Title.

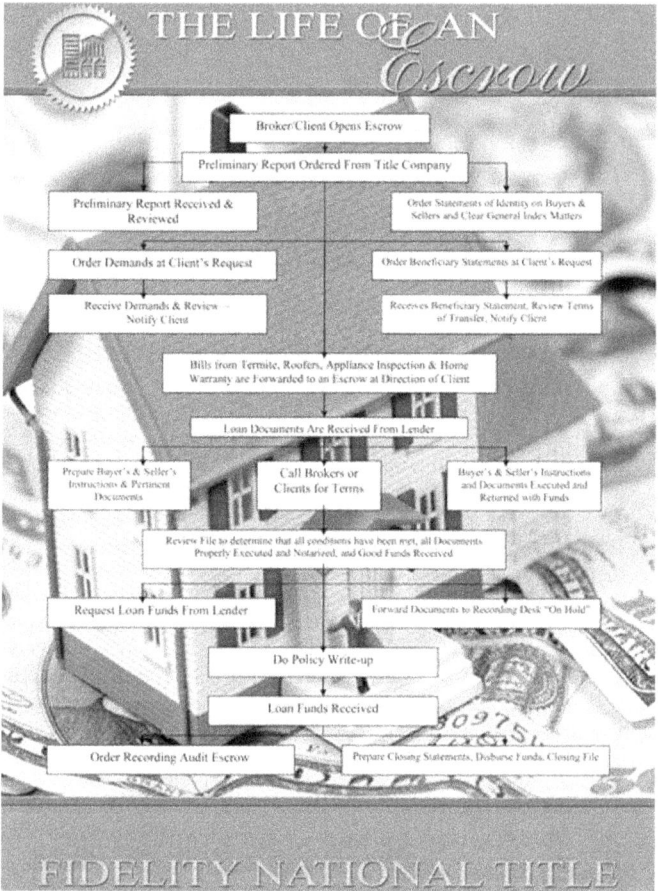

Acting as a neutral third party, the escrow company provides the following services:

- ✓ Collects the required funds from all parties

- ✓ Compiles all the documents in the closing process
- ✓ Serves as a non-biased 3rd party
- ✓ Provides an accounting of all funds
- ✓ Responds to requests from the principals
- ✓ Advises buyers of the vesting options available with the final decision being in the hands of the buyer
- ✓ Produces the Closing or Settlement Statement
- ✓ Provides notary services
- ✓ Disburses funds
- ✓ Records documents

All of the above services are done in accordance with the contractually-agreed upon conditions of the transacting parties.

Some of the common mistakes that Buyers make that slow or stop an escrow transaction according to Candice Hoover, Account Manager of Fidelity National Title Company are:

- ➢ The Buyer does not have the additional funds needed to close transaction
- ➢ The buyer brings a personal check for closing
- ➢ Husband/wife comes to sign without spouse
- ➢ Escrow Officer was not aware of marriage, separation, divorce, sole and

separate property, death of a joint tenant, etc., making all papers incorrect

- ➢ One of the spouses is out of town
- ➢ Buyer signs loan papers incorrectly
- ➢ Judgments arise during escrow period
- ➢ Buyer does not have proper info for notary
- ➢ Buyers make a major purchase on Credit

In addition to the above common buyer hurdles, there are also several other issues from lenders, sellers, insurance providers and inspection providers that could slow or stop the escrow process. Make sure that your Realtor obtains the services of an established, well respected Title Company or Closing Attorney to facilitate a smooth and timely closing.

CHAPTER 10

TAKING TITLE TO THE HOME

*Owning a home is the culmination of many years of hard work and the realization of the American Dream. - **Solomon Ortiz***

There are several different ways of taking title to your new home. Different life circumstances may constitute taking title in a different way than you have in the past. Title may be taken in the following ways:

1. Sole ownership
2. Tenancy in Common
3. Joint Tenancy
4. Community Property or Partnership interests
5. Ownership by other lawfully created entities

Wow! If you weren't confused before then you probably are now. Don't worry, the closing Attorney or Title Company can help you select the most appropriate choice for you. I'll outline some of the major characteristics of each. However, please consult with a professional before making a decision as your choice will dictate what happens to the property in the event of your death or, in some cases, your incapacitation. This subject is one that you don't want to think about but something that you must decide upon.

1. **Sole ownership**

   Sole ownership pertains to just one person as owner. It is defined to mean ownership by one person being the sole owner who enjoys the benefits of the property and is subject to the accompanying burdens, such as the payment of taxes. The sole owner is free to sell the property at will.

2. **Tenancy in Common**

   Tenancy in common exists when several, two or more, persons are owners of property. One person may hold a 20% interest in the property, one a 35% interest and one a 45% interest. In other words, each person can hold a differing percentage of interest. There is a unity of possession which means that each owner has the right to possession. An owner can't charge another owner rent for the use of the property unless agreed upon by all parties. This is of course subject to applicable federal and state law. A tenant in common is free to sell, transfer or otherwise convey or mortgage the tenant's own interest as he or she sees fit.

Be very careful about this type of ownership because no right of survivorship exists. So when someone dies, their interest passes to their beneficiaries according to their will. I've seen this type of ownership used in cases where spouses have both been married before with children from previous marriages and they want their share to go to their own children rather than to pass to the surviving spouse.

3. Joint Tenancy

Joint tenancy is probably the most common ownership type used. It means that each owner must have the same ownership interest whether it is two people or more than two people. To establish joint tenancy, a fourfold unity must exist: interest, title, time and possession. Owners have the same interest, acquired by the same conveyance, commencing at the same time and held by the same possession.

The most important characteristic of joint tenancy is the right of survivorship that flows from the unity of interest. If one joint tenant dies, the surviving joint tenant becomes the owner of the property. In the case of several surviving joint tenants, the interest is split jointly between all the surviving joint tenants. Joint tenancy property cannot be sold or disposed of by the last will and testament and does not become part of the estate of a joint tenant subject to probate. Furthermore, the surviving joint tenant or tenants are not liable to creditors of the deceased who only hold existing liens on the joint tenancy property.

4. **Community Property or Partnership Interests**

Community Property or Partnership interests ownership is not available in all states, 9 states as of this writing, so please check with your attorney before making decisions regarding this form of ownership. Community Property generally consists of property acquired by a husband and wife or by either one of them during a valid marriage. Separate property may also fall into this category, but you will have to obtain legal advice on this. California is a community property state. In addition, the laws regarding civil unions are evolving and can be a factor that you need to consider.

5. **Ownership by other lawfully created entities**

Entities can be Corporations, LLC's, Trusts, Non-profits and many, many others. This is not a very common ownership type so check with your attorney if this is something that might interest you.

CHAPTER 11

SHOULD I PURCHASE A HOME WARRANTY?

"Warranties are a matter of risk assessment. Are you willing to take the risk" – **Dan Craddock**

This is a decision that you will ultimately have to make when purchasing a home. Personally, I like home warranties and think everyone should have one. When purchasing brand new construction, you get a home warranty automatically. Why then shouldn't you have one for a home that has some miles on it and may really have some problems?

What does a home warranty cover? The simple answer is that it can cover everything or just a few things depending on the policy that you purchase. There are several good companies offering home warranties and you can research them on the internet. What you will find is that each one is different and has policies that cover different things. They might have different levels of coverage or allow you to add specific items to a basic package, so you will need to do your own research.

In my opinion, home warranty companies purposely offer different coverage's in a basic package in order to make it difficult to compare policies between companies. As a result, it may take some time to determine what the differences in coverage's are between the basic packages of several different home warranty companies. What warranties will not cover universally are such things as permit or hauling fees, cosmetic structures such as oven rotisseries, broiling and baking attachments, refrigerator shelves and bins and water filtering devices. Warranties also do not cover any structural problems in your home such as cracks in the walls or a leaky roof.

Here are a few things you should expect from a home warranty Company:

- Courteous service representatives who are trained to help solve your problems over the phone, if possible

- Local, licensed, insured, dependable and pre-screened technicians (this is a must)

- Guaranteed service work – without an additional service fee (expect at least 30 days labor and 90 days parts)

- An Excellent track record of performance.

Some things that are covered under the warranty may not be repaired or replaced by the home warranty company if the appliances or systems had pre-existing problems at the time that you obtained the warranty. In addition, the home warranty Company may not be willing to repair items that were improperly maintained or installed or that violate building codes.

While the choices between coverage levels of different home warranty companies may seem overwhelming, my recommendation is to have the seller provide a one year home warranty covering all major appliances, heating and cooling systems, and plumbing and electrical systems.

The bottom line is that a home warranty can be worth your while and save you thousands of dollars. Remember, it is an insurance policy so you'll only realize how good or bad your choice was if you have a problem and need to utilize the warranty.

CHAPTER 12

CHINESE DRYWALL

"You can measure opportunity with the same yardstick that measures the risk involved. They go together." - **Earl Nightingale**

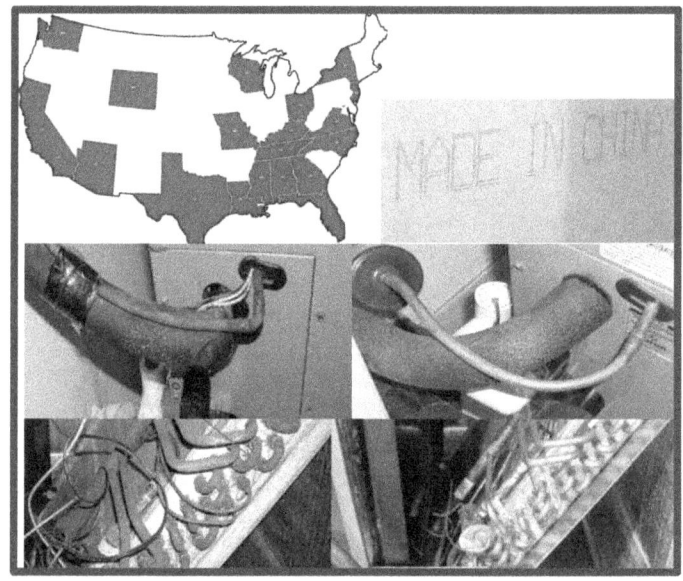

By now, most people have heard of Chinese drywall but very few know exactly what it is or why they should be concerned with it. Is it only in Florida or is it in other states also? Should I have a home inspected for Chinese drywall? The bottom line is that you SHOULD BE CONCERNED. Chinese drywall could be in any house that you are considering anywhere in the United States. Virtually all homes built in the US use drywall for the walls and ceilings. Most of the Chinese drywall has been found in Florida, but there are cases in many other states.

Chinese drywall, also known as wallboard, gypsum board or plaster board, was imported from China starting in 2001. The drywall is made of waste materials and some believe that the humidity in the air causes the sulfur in the drywall to give off a gas which creates the noxious odor. This odor smells like rotten eggs but the main problem with the Chinese drywall is that it will corrode copper plumbing, copper electrical wiring, copper water lines as well as other metals like chrome, brass and silver. Usually the air conditioning coils are the first to turn black as well as any exposed copper piping.

How do I check for Chinese drywall? An inspection by a professional Chinese drywall inspector is suggested but prior to having an inspection there are some things that you can check for yourself. As I mentioned earlier, check the air conditioning coils as well as the exposed copper piping on the coils. Also check copper fittings under the sinks. Another thing to check is the copper ground wire in the receptacles. Only do this if the power is OFF. Rub your finger across the copper and if the black stuff comes off on your finger then you can be assured that you have some type of problem that needs to be checked out by a professional.

One way that people check for Chinese drywall is to go up into the attic and check the stamp on the back of the drywall. If it says 'Made in China' or 'Chinese drywall' then you can be assured that you have a problem. The problem with this is that some US re-sellers of the drywall were rebranding the Chinese drywall with their own name so you really don't know if you have it.

If the house doesn't have a sulfur smell, am I assured that the home doesn't have Chinese drywall? The short answer is NO. The builder or remodeler might have only used one sheet or a few sheets of Chinese drywall so the home might not have the classic rotten egg smell. This is where a professional Chinese drywall inspector may be the only way to determine if you have Chinese drywall in your home.

Should I buy a home that has been totally remediated from Chinese drywall? Depending on where you live, there may be laws governing how the remediation is to be done and what is to be remediated. At one time they said that all the wiring had to be replaced which is very expensive. They have since changed this to require only a certain portion of the wiring. If you are going to purchase one of these remediated houses then I would check with your county building department to see what the rules are and what they had to inspect to get a Certificate of Occupancy (COO). After you have this information then you can make an informed decision. One of the main advantages of purchasing a remediated home is to save money since these homes are usually sold at a discount.

CHAPTER 13

BUYING A FORECLOSURE OR REO

"Look at market fluctuations as your friend rather than your enemy; profit from folly rather than participate in it." - **Warren Buffett**

Foreclosures are defined as homes that have gone back to the lender because the homeowner could not pay the mortgage. What does foreclosure mean to you?   Great deal?

Lowest price in the neighborhood? A lot of home for a little money? A chance to make a killing in real estate? This question has been asked over and over again because we have so many foreclosures. Foreclosures have been around ever since home loans have been around but it's only now that they are a hot button for the general public. Investors have been buying foreclosures or Real Estate Owned (REO) (which is the term used for foreclosed homes owned by banks or other financial institutions), for years so it's nothing new for them. If you've ever thought about becoming an investor and taken a course given by one of the so-called real estate guru's, you've been schooled in buying foreclosures and/or REO's.

There are many variables that go into establishing the prices for these homes so you'll need work with your Realtor to determine the market value. You purchase these homes just like you would any other home on the market.

You might have seen HUD homes on the market. These are homes that are owned by the US Department of Housing and Urban Development. HUD homes are foreclosures but the process to purchase a HUD home is very different from the typical foreclosure. For one thing, your Realtor, along with their broker, must be registered with HUD in order to enter a bid for you? And, yes you have to bid for these homes. If you are going to purchase a HUD home, make sure that your Realtor has done this before and is well versed in the process.

HUD homes are sold AS IS so the onus is on you to have inspections done to determine if there are any structural or other costly issues with the property. These HUD properties are controlled by an asset management Company. This asset management company will determine whether the electricity and water can be turned on so you can have your inspections done.

I had a case where the asset management company said we couldn't turn on the water but the buyer was adamant on moving ahead with the deal. We determined that the only problem was that the hose for the ice maker was stuck in the wall so the water would leak into the wall when the water was turned on. This was an easy fix and thus a good deal for the buyers. The HUD buying process is very specific and if you don't do everything right in the specified time frame then your bid will be rejected. However, if you find out that you can't have the water or electricity turned on then you might want to pass on this home.

The HUD buying process is very specific and if you don't do everything right in the specified time frame, your bid will be rejected.

Also, beware of bidding more than the offer price as you'll have to come up with this amount of your bid that exceeds the offering price as part of your down payment. If the HUD home is in great condition, I advise my buyers to bid at least $100.00 or more over the asking price if they are really serious about getting the home. Check with your Realtor to determine if this is something that you want to pursue and what the ramifications are.

Here are my seven tips for purchasing Foreclosures or REO's:

1. **Choose a Realtor that has experience with Foreclosures**

   All foreclosures are not created equal and a Realtor that is experienced with a variety of foreclosures is a must. Also, make sure that they are registered with HUD.

2. **Find out the Property History**

   Have your Realtor find out when the property was foreclosed on and how much the lender paid for the home. Also have them check how much the previous owner had purchased the property for. This information as well as the type of market that you are in, either a buyer's or seller's market, will help you formulate your offer.

3. Determine the Comparable Sales in the Area

Have your Realtor do a Comparative Market Analysis (CMA), which will show you the homes that are on the market, the homes that are under contract or pending and the homes that have sold usually in a ½ mile radius of the home. This will give you an idea of how this foreclosure is priced as well as whether homes are selling in this area. Having this information is essential before you place an offer.

4. Check for Tax and other Liens

A foreclosed home may have back taxes owed or other liens against it. Bank owned homes or REO's have the least risk for buyers looking for foreclosed homes. When a bank owns a foreclosed property there are no taxes or liens and the property is vacant. However, have your Realtor double check since this one little detail could cost you thousands of dollars.

5. Have Inspections Done

I can't emphasize this enough. Have a licensed inspector do a thorough home inspection. Before you choose an inspector tell them you want to be there as they inspect the home. If they are not comfortable with this then get another inspector. Bring a video camera, paper, pen and flashlight. Have the inspector explain how certain things work and film it. Odds are that you won't remember everything the inspector tells you so the video will come in handy for future reference. By filming the attic and the basement, you will have a baseline if things go awry years down the road. You can then compare what it looked like when you purchased the home versus the present condition.

6. **Don't ask the REO company to pay for any repairs**

Lenders will look at offers on a NET BASIS to determine which one they will accept. When making an offer you are welcome to ask the seller pay to a portion of the closing costs as well as any repairs that might be needed. However, by doing so you will almost guarantee that someone else wins the bid. The lender will always choose the offer that nets them or gives them the most money. Again, check with your Realtor for advice.

7. **Expect an AS IS Sale**

Foreclosures are sold on an AS IS basis which means that what you see is what you get. The seller is unlikely to agree to repair or replace items. In the case of a home in bad condition that has been on the market for an extended period of time, the seller may make an exception and offer concessions just to get the home off their books. It's buyer beware, so be sure that you know what you are doing.

CHAPTER 14

BUYING A SHORT SALE

"Markets always change, and as soon as there's downturn, cleanliness becomes a major value." - **Donald Trump**

You might have heard horror stories about short sales or you might know someone that has purchased one, but do you really have a full understanding of what a short sale is? Someone that is doing a short sale on their home is selling the home for less than they owe on their mortgage loan or loans. They might have bought the home at the height of the market and now their home is worth less than they paid for it. The home is still owned by the seller but the lender will be the one that has the final approval on the short sale since they will be the one who takes the loss.

At first, banks were, without exception, unwilling to accept lower prices for these homes. Then they started coming around and would accept a lower price if the current owner would agree to share in the loss. Since most homeowners in this situation don't have cash to put towards the loss, the lender would agree to accept a certain amount of money in monthly installments. Banks are willing to negotiate the amount and even the installment period. I've been able to cut the total amount in half and even double the installment length just by negotiating with the bank.

Short sales are becoming more prevalent in the marketplace and the good thing is that banks are willing to negotiate. Today, banks realize that foreclosing on these properties and adding them to their large number of non-producing assets on their books is not in their best interest financially. Short sales negotiations between the bank and the homeowner / prospective buyer used to take between six to nine months and usually did not result in a sale. Lately we've seen short sales closing in as little as a few weeks as banks try to clear their inventory of REOs. Hopefully this trend will continue.

Does this mean that I should consider buying a short sale? I would definitely consider purchasing a short sale as you can usually get the home for less than market value. Of course, this depends on the condition of the property and the demand for such properties in your market. I've had some short sales sell for well over the list price due to increased demand for a home that was move-in ready. While the timeframe for a short sale has been reduced considerably, there are still cases where a short sale just doesn't work. This occurs usually when there are several owners of the mortgage debt and they can't get all of them to agree.

What questions should I ask my Realtor before I make an offer on a short sale? The first question to ask is: has the lender agreed to a price? If so, then this is the best position you can be in. If not, then you'll ask the following question: how far along in the process is the short sale? The further along it is then the better off you are. Your Realtor should find out whether the owner has a hardship or not, how many loans are outstanding on the home and, in the case of multiple loans on the home, are the loans with the same institution. The best case scenario is only one loan on the home. The next best scenario is if there are two loans on the home and they are with the same lender. If there are two loans and they are with different lenders then negotiations will be a lot tougher since you have to get both lenders to agree to the offer.

Another thing your Realtor needs to find out is whether the loan is now owned by a group of investors. Let me explain briefly. Loans made by lenders are often sold on the back end to other lenders, insurance companies, pension funds, groups of investors, etc. They are typically packaged in a bundle with other loans and sold to groups. The worst case scenario is if a loan was sold to a group of investors. If so, then all the investors must agree on the short sale or it doesn't work. Simply put, the more people that have to agree with the terms of the short sale, the more it increases the likelihood that the deal will fail.

The HUD-1 Settlement Statement is a standard form used to itemize services and fees charged and/or credited to the borrower as well as the itemized charges and credits to the seller. The entire deal, all charges and credits associated with the deal, has to be listed on the HUD-1 statement and there cannot be any payments made to anyone outside of escrow. Reject any deal that requires a payment outside of escrow as this is a red flag that something may not be ethical or legal.

CHAPTER 15

BUYING A SELLER FINANCED HOME

"Never count on making a good sale. Have the purchase price be so attractive that even a mediocre sale gives good results." - **Warren Buffett**

While it is very rare to find a house with seller financing, also called Owner Financing, it is a possibility and something that you might consider. If your credit is less than stellar, this might be a good option for you to pursue. Seller financing can come in the form of a first or second mortgage and can offer different terms, much like lender financing does. In fact, sellers are oftentimes willing to be more creative on financing in order to close a deal. There are some precautions that you should be aware of that will be explained later. The following are several reasons why a seller will offer financing:

1. Reduce the time to sell the home.

The Seller may need cash or may have a pressing reason to sell the house quickly and this is a great way for a seller to accomplish that.

2. The Seller is having trouble selling the house and has to provide some incentive to the buyer.

The home might has been on the market for a long period of time and the seller is unwilling to reduce the price so the only other incentive is to provide financing. This will likely attract buyers that don't quite qualify for a traditional mortgage or have a pressing need to get into a home quickly.

3. As a strategy for a Hard to Finance Property.

There are several types of properties that might fall into this category, such as mixed use property, undeveloped land, mobile home and land, non-conforming properties and low value properties. Investors are especially interested in these types of properties as they can buy them at a discount and flip them at a retail price with favorable financing terms.

There are also situations where work might have been done on the home that was not properly permitted like adding a bedroom or enclosing a garage, etc. The home will have a difficult time passing a property inspection and thus obtaining financing. This could be just the property you are looking for but be careful not to sacrifice short term gain with long term suffering. It might be nice now but when you are ready to sell, you will have the same problems as the previous seller unless you are able to rectify the permitting issues. A good Realtor can advise you of the ramifications.

4. The Seller is looking for a steady income stream.

   When bank interest rates are at 1% or less, it makes sense to offer seller financing at 6% or higher. The seller is getting more money than they can obtain from a bank deposit and they get a steady stream of income. The seller is willing to take a risk by getting a substantial down payment and a higher than market interest rate.

As you can see, there are many reasons why a seller chooses to offer financing on their property. There are individuals offering financing on their own home but mostly it's investors trying to maximize their return. Investors offer financing because it benefits them, so make sure you understand fully the terms of their offer before entering into any agreement. In addition to the down payment, most investors will charge you "points" upfront. A point is equivalent to 1% of the outstanding loan amount. Typically, investors will charge anywhere from 3 to 7 points upfront just to give you the loan. In an environment where interest rates are under 4%, it doesn't make much sense to pay these fees. In addition, the seller will charge an interest rate based on risk. If you cannot get approved for a traditional mortgage from a mortgage broker or banker, it is likely that you are at a higher risk for default than the average borrower. In order for the seller to be comfortable in taking the risk, they will likely charge points as well as a higher interest rate. Usually, interest rates for seller financing will range from 2% to 8% above the average mortgage interest rate. This is dependent on the seller and how much of a risk they are willing to take.

If you hear the seller talking about a "balloon", pay careful attention. Often the sellers are not willing to wait 15 or 30 years for their money so they will incorporate a "balloon" payment which is the term used to describe a lump sum payment that is due before the stated term of the loan. For example, if the seller says that they will give you a 30 year loan with a 5 year balloon then he is saying that the monthly payment will be calculated based upon a 30 year term but the outstanding loan balance will be due in a lump sum payment at the end of 5 years.

It's always a gamble if you can refinance the home before the five years is up. Home prices might go down, you might lose your job, your identity might get stolen and your credit score trashed. Any number of things could occur that you didn't foresee when you entered into the original agreement. It's best to get a 15 or 30 year loan so you don't have to worry about having to refinance. In the reverse, home prices could go way up and you could have built up a substantial equity position in the home meaning that refinancing could be easier.

While seller financing has some benefits, you also need to be aware of the pitfalls. There have been situations where a seller has sold their home with financing only to have the home foreclosed on a short time later due to unpaid liens. To avoid this and many other such situations, you need to utilize the services of a Title Company or Attorney. With a Title Company, you will get Title Insurance that will protect you if the Title to the home has some issues. Be very leery of the seller that wants to handle the entire transaction on their own promising you very favorable terms.

To summarize, the characteristics of the typical seller financed home is upfront points, an interest rate higher than the average going rate and a balloon note of 3, 5 or 7 years. A seller financed home might have one or several of these characteristics so make sure you are aware of all the terms of the proposed loan and the associated risks.

CHAPTER 16

LEASE OPTIONS OR RENT TO OWN

"Risk comes from not knowing what you're doing." – **Warren Buffett**

You might have heard one or both of these terms before, but they mean the exact same thing. A lease option is an option to purchase a home at a specified period of time. It is for individuals and families that want to own their own home, but for some reason have not been able to qualify using the traditional channels. The lease option can be incorporated with a rental agreement, but it is best to have two separate agreements. The lessee, the person wanting to purchase the home, will rent a home for a period of time with an option to purchase the home at a set time and, in some cases, a set price. There are many variations to a lease option so be diligent in your review of the terms.

The lease option usually consists of an upfront option fee plus a monthly option premium. The upfront option fee, the security deposit and most of the monthly option premium will typically go towards the down payment on the home. However, this is not always the case so make sure you are familiar with all the terms before entering into the agreement.

The term of the lease option is usually a year or two but it could be as many as 3 to 5 years. Investors will ask for as short an option as they can get the borrower to agree to because they want to get their money out of the property as quickly as possible. The monthly rent payment is usually the going rate for the property and the monthly option premium varies (can be as low as $50 or much higher).

If at the end of the option period the buyer does not exercise the option, the upfront option fee as well as the monthly option premiums already paid to date are forfeited to the seller.

It is easy to see why investors love to do lease options! In many cases, due to buyers not properly exercising their options, they can do them over and over again on the same property. How do they get away with this? Let me explain, a buyer enters into this type of arrangement because they either don't have the credit score to get a traditional mortgage or they don't have enough money for a down payment. Most often it's both. During the option period, the buyer is paying an option premium on top of their rent, so they are usually not able to save any additional money for the down payment. When the option expiration dates arrives, the buyer must qualify for a traditional mortgage in order to pay off the investor. Even if the upfront option fee plus the total of all monthly option premiums paid are all applied to the mortgage, it will typically not be enough to cover the required 80% loan-to-value in order to get a traditional mortgage. In this case, the borrower is unable to exercise the options and forfeits all the additional monies they paid toward the option.

Now, let's discuss the purchase price of the home. I've seen the purchase price calculated a couple of different ways and, depending on the type of market, one will usually work better than the other. The first way is for the seller to establish the sales price upfront, which, depending on the length of the option, will likely be higher than the current market price of the home. For example, if home prices are increasing at an annualized 5% rate and the option is for 2 years, the seller might price the home 10% above the current market price. The other way to price the home is to average out the values of two different appraisals (completed by two independent companies that have been mutually agreed upon by the buyer and seller) performed a couple of months before the option expires.

Whichever method is used, make sure that it is documented in the lease option agreement along with language dictating what is to be done should the home not appraise for the agreed upon selling price. You need to cover your bases upfront instead of waiting until it's time to exercise the option and find out it won't work for you.

CHAPTER 17

FINAL THOUGHTS

"A man complained that [on] his way home to dinner he had every day to pass through that long field of his neighbor's. I advised him to buy it, and it would never seem long again."
-Ralph Waldo Emerson

Home ownership is still the dream that most Americans strive for. It is a safe haven. It provides security for your family and solace in inflationary times. Throughout history real estate has been one of the best methods of attaining personal wealth. Real estate has cycles and prices go up in good times and down in bad times. The objective is to buy at the bottom of the cycle and sell at the top. This is very difficult to do because once you realize that you are at the top or bottom, the market has usually turned the other way. Momentum is another variable that is hard to go against. When the market is going up, more people are interested in buying and when the market is going down, more people panic and sell.

Home ownership is also a personal choice. If you've ever owned your own home then you will not want to go back to being a renter again. Owning a home provides a sense of stability that you don't experience while renting. In fact, renting may make things in your life feel more temporary. As a result, I always recommend owning over renting if you can afford it – the benefits are simply too numerous.

 As I said before, Real Estate goes in cycles and we've recently been through the down cycle. It's now time to reap the rewards of low housing prices and low interest rates. Mark my words, this market will not happen again in our lifetimes and it's best to lock in a low price and a low interest rate while you still have the chance.

I hope you have enjoyed this book and it has helped you in your quest for a home. It's now up to you. Make it happen!

If I can be of service to you, please don't hesitate to contact me at d_craddock@yahoo.com.

Good Luck and Be Prosperous!

CHAPTER 18

BONUS – CREDIT INFORMATION

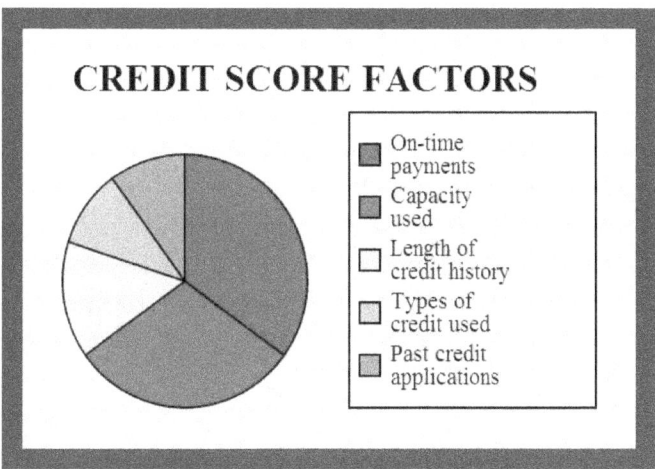

CREDIT SCORE FACTORS

- On-time payments
- Capacity used
- Length of credit history
- Types of credit used
- Past credit applications

This chapter alone is worth far more than the cost of this book. Following the tips presented can potentially save you hundreds of thousands of dollars during your lifetime which is what compelled me to include the information as part of the book. Enjoy the journey.

Your credit score is a number that summarizes your credit risk based on a snapshot of your credit report at a particular point in time. Basically, the higher your credit score, the better chance you have of getting approved for a loan. In addition, a high credit score can save you money when purchasing homeowners insurance, car insurance, applying for an auto loan, personal loans or a mortgage refinance. It can even have an effect on job opportunities. Yes, employers are looking at your credit score as a determining factor when hiring new employees.

You might have heard about the three credit bureaus that provide your credit score to lenders. These three credit bureaus are Experian in Allen, Texas; Equifax in Atlanta, Georgia; and TransUnion in Chester Pennsylvania. Depending on the area of the country that you live in, one or more of these bureaus will be the dominant ones. Why is this so? Lenders don't always provide information to all the credit bureaus thus the difference in the scores. Which score do lenders use? Since the three scores may vary by as little as a few points to much more, lenders usually use the middle score. However, there may be exceptions. Credit scores range from a low of 300 to a high of 850. I haven't been able to find out why these particular numbers were chosen but needless to say, the higher score the better.

Each of the three credit reporting agencies has a different name for your credit or FICO score as follows but they all mean the same thing:

> Equifax – Beacon score
> Experian – Experian/FICO Risk Model

> TransUnion – FICO Risk Score, Classic

FICO, formally Fair, Isaac and Company, is a public company founded in 1956 that provides decision making and analytic services including credit scoring. Originally, your FICO or credit score was used primarily when applying for mortgages and other such loans. The use of credit scores has expanded so that your credit score is utilized for just about everything where risk is a factor. If you think monitoring your credit and ensuring that your credit score is kept in the upper ranges is a difficult task or one you just don't want to do, consider this. When you consider that the difference between a high and medium credit score for a mortgage loan can cost you hundreds of thousands of dollars over the course of the loan, it's definitely worth it.

Whether you apply for a mortgage, auto loan, credit card or personal loan, lenders want to know how likely it is that they will be paid back. In other words, what is your credit risk? Both positive and negative data regarding prior credit patterns can be found at the credit bureaus. Most lenders incorporate credit scores into making credit decisions so your credit score or prior credit performance will influence the credit offers you receive in the mail or by email.

How is your credit score calculated?

Over the years, the FICO or credit score calculation has undergone many changes. The current credit score is called FICO 8 and there will most likely be additional iterations in the future as people devise ways to get around the system like trade line renting which I will explain later. The major changes have to do with:

> High credit card usage – If you have a credit card with a balance that is close to the card's limit then you will likely lose more points than in previous iterations. Keeping balances low on credit cards is now a must.

> Isolated late payments – If your accounts are kept in good standing and you have a 30 day late that is an isolated incident, the effects on your credit score will not be as severe as previous FICO calculations. However, if the late payment is not isolated and your credit shows a history of late payments then the reverse is true and you will lose more points.

> Authorized user of credit card – The formula utilized by the credit bureaus has always allowed the use of adding authorized users to credit card accounts to help users increase their credit score from shared management of an account. However, the advantage in

FICO 8 scoring has been reduced because of the practice of trade line renting which has to do with adding a person's name to another's credit card for the sole purpose of raising their credit score. This practice does not change the risk to the lender and so the FICO 8 score takes this into account.

➢ Small balance collections accounts – When the original balance on an account was less than $100, any collections associated with these accounts, deemed nuisance collections, are ignored in the scoring model for FICO 8.

There are over three hundred total characteristics that have been determined as having an impact on your credit risk. Of these three hundred, they have identified a core group of forty characteristics which represent the most predictive characteristics used to calculate your credit score. Those things that are considered include:

➢ Trade lines (defined as accounts reported to the credit bureaus)
➢ Inquiries
➢ Collections
➢ Public Records

There are also specific characteristics that are not considered which include:

- ☒ Age
- ☒ Address
- ☒ Employment
- ☒ Income
- ☒ Gender

There are five categories of predictive characteristics that the credit bureaus utilize to calculate your credit score which are:

- ✓ Payment History
- ✓ Outstanding Debt
- ✓ Credit History Length
- ✓ Pursuit of New Credit
- ✓ Credit Mix

Each of these five categories carry a specific weight or is calculated utilizing a specific percentage. The main factors as well as the percentage weight of each category are presented below.

1. Payment History – 35%
   a. How recent have you had a delinquency, collection or public record item?
   b. How severe was the worst delinquency i.e. was it 30 days late or 90 days late?
   c. How many credit obligations have been delinquent?
2. Outstanding Debt – 30%

a. How much does the consumer owe creditors or what is the consumers total outstanding debt?

b. What percentage of available credit card limits is the consumer using? In other words, if a consumer has a total credit limit on all credit cards of $1,000 and has a total balance of $400 then the percentage would be 40%.

c. What percentage is outstanding on open installment loans? For example, if the original mortgage was $100,000 and a car loan was $10,000 and you now owe $50,000 and $5,000, then your percentage owed is 50%.

3. <u>Credit History Length</u> – 15%

a. How long have accounts been established – average number of months accounts have been open. The longer the accounts have been open, the less the risk. Conversely, if the accounts are very new then the risk is high even though you might have a high credit limit.

b. New accounts – the number of months since the most recent account has been opened. Again, the longer your accounts have been open, the better. It is never a good idea to open a new account when you are in the market for a home.

4. Pursuit of New Credit – 10%
    a. The number of recent inquiries in the last 12 months
    b. The number of new trade lines opened in the last year
5. Credit Mix – 10%
    a. What is the mix of credit product types? How many credit cards, installment loans, etc.
    b. Revolving credit – How many open credit cards do you have?
    c. Installment credit – What is the percent of accounts that are installment loans?

Why doesn't everyone have a credit score? There are some people that choose to pay cash for everything and don't have any credit cards or loans and thus no credit score. While this is very admirable and should be encouraged, there may be the occasion where you need to purchase something on credit. So, if you don't have a credit score, it will take a while to establish a score.   Here are the minimum criteria for having a credit score:

➤ The consumer must be alive (Obviously)

- ➢ One account must be open at least six months
- ➢ One undisputed account must be updated in the last six months. In other words, there must have been some activity on the account that requires the creditor to send an update to the credit bureau.

Even if you don't believe in having debt, it is wise to have a credit card, a mortgage or other installment loan. There may be an unforeseen circumstance like a sudden medical problem, a legal issue or an investment with a fantastic return on investment (ROI) that will require you to obtain a loan in a relatively short period of time. Without a credit score, you may be at a huge disadvantage that could be very costly to you. These types of situations can't be predicted but a little advance preparation can make a big difference in the outcome.

Now that you have a basic understanding of how your credit score is calculated, let's talk about how certain events affect your credit and how long certain events remain on your credit report and thus affect your credit score? First of all, the event I'm referring to is a negative action to your credit report like a payment that is 30 days late, a foreclosure, a bankruptcy, etc. Having said this, the aforementioned questions are not easy to answer. The simple answer is that the higher your credit score is before the event is recorded on your credit report, the more it will affect your actual credit score after the event occurs. For example, someone with an 820 credit score that has a 30 day late payment with result in a greater point drop than someone starting with a 680 credit score. In other words, the higher your credit score is before the event, the harder it will fall after the event.

How does a Short Sale, a Foreclosure or Bankruptcy affect your credit score and how long will it remain on your credit report? This too depends on your starting credit score. The higher the initial credit score, the more effect the event will have on your score. Beware of anyone that says a certain event will affect your credit score by a specific number of points without actually analyzing your particular situation.

You'll also want to know how long it takes to recover from an event like a payment that is thirty day late, a short sale, a foreclosure or a bankruptcy. This depends on your initial credit score before the event happened. With a low starting credit score, a thirty day late payment may affect your credit score for under a year whereas if you are in the highest FICO score bracket, the effects can last for many years. In the case of a short sale, foreclosure or a deed in lieu, the effects can last around three years to around seven years depending on your credit score before the event was reported to the credit bureau.

How Do You Rebuild Your Credit?

Now that you know what makes up your credit score and how it is calculated, how do you rebuild your credit or maintain your good credit? The first thing you have to do is focus on the issue and not leave it to chance. Some people have a great income but have made some poor choices where their credit is concerned or they were lax or forgetful when paying their bills. The following tips are really common sense but require time, effort and focus to keep on top of them:

- ✓ Check your Credit Report for errors – Request a free copy annually of your credit report from **annualcreditreport.com** and check it for errors or omissions. Specifically check for payment inaccuracies especially focusing on late payments. Make sure that the amounts owed on open accounts are correct and ensure that all your accounts have been reported. If you discover errors, dispute them in writing with the credit bureau and reporting entity. Each credit bureau has a specific dispute reporting process but all of them require that disputes be submitting in writing.

- ✓ Setup Payment Reminders – Making on-time payments is one of the biggest contributing factors to your credit score. Also consider enrolling in automatic payments with your bank, credit union or other institution so that payments are automatically debited from your account each month.

- ✓ Reduce the Amount of Debt you owe – Develop a payment plan that puts most of your available budget for debt payments towards the highest interest cards or loans first while paying minimum payments on your other accounts. In other words, if you have two credit cards, one with an 8% interest rate and one with a 16% interest rate, it is better to pay the minimum on the lower rate card and pay as much as you can afford on the higher rate card so you can pay it off sooner. It is also important that you don't skip a payment on one account so that you can pay more on another.

- ✓ Pay your bills on time – This sounds so simple yet is one of the hardest things to do if you don't have the right focus and a system to keep track of your finances.
- ✓ If you inadvertently miss a payment, get current and remain current. Sometimes things just happen but don't let it happen more than once.
- ✓ Keep balances low on credit cards – For instance, if you have two credit cards with a $1,000 limit on each, it's best to owe 50% on each card than to owe 100% on one of the cards. Keep the balances low according to your credit limit.
- ✓ Closing an account with previous missed payments or paying off a collection account will not remove it from your credit report
- ✓ If you are having trouble making your payments, contact your lender or a qualified credit counselor. Utilizing a credit counselor will not affect your credit score.
- ✓ Pay off rather than move debt around – This is what many people do when they receive offers of new credit cards with no interest or low interest for a period of time. It is better to pay off the debt than open a

new credit line and move the debt around.

✓ Don't close unused credit cards in an attempt to raise your score – This will actually work in reverse as it will reduce your total overall credit amount and increase the percentage that you owe on your remaining credit.

✓ Don't open a number of new accounts in an attempt to raise your credit score – If you don't have any credit then you need to establish credit but if you already have established credit then any new accounts will increase your risk to a lender.

✓ If you have a short credit history, avoid opening a lot of credit lines at one time – Credit takes time to mature and you'll have to wait it out and open credit lines at certain intervals so that your risk assessment is not adversely affected. Every time you open a new credit line, you can expect it to have some effect on your credit score but over time these accounts will mature and turn into a positive.

✓ Avoid utilizing credit repair agencies that charge you a fee to improve your credit score – There are many legitimate credit repair agencies available to use that don't charge you an upfront fee.

Credit Counseling is an option that you may want to consider depending on your particular situation. As I mentioned previously, seeking assistance from a credit counselor WILL NOT negatively impact a consumer's credit score. Actually, informed consumers generally have higher credit scores. As you know, a good credit score is a prerequisite to qualify for a mortgage.

This chapter has provided information as to how your credit score is used, how your credit score is calculated and how to increase, rebuild or maintain your credit score. After reading and digesting the information, you are now in the top 10% of all consumers. It is critical to get a copy of your credit report every year, to dispute any discrepancies, to keep your accounts current, to re-read this chapter often and to maintain a focus on your credit score. You owe it to yourself and those that depend on you. Use it wisely and prosper.

COMMON SENSE GUIDES

This is the first in a series of Common Sense Books designed to provide you with sound and practical advice. Be on the lookout for future Books.

www.ingramcontent.com/pod-product-compliance
Lightning Source LLC
Chambersburg PA
CBHW051547170526
45165CB00002B/916